The Sound of English
pronunciation
by Joseph Hudson

PUBLISHING

Published by Anouka Ltd.
Basement 37 Gray's Inn Rd,
London,
WC1X 8PQ

www.thesoundofenglish.org

First Edition 2018

ISBN 978-1-9164822-3-4

English pronunciation is not one skill.

It is three: **producing** sounds, **selecting** sounds, and **joining** sounds together.

This new edition of 'The Sound of English' uses the same practical approach we have developed at Pronunciation Studio in London to tackle these areas of English speech that are often ignored in general English lessons.

The course is designed to take learners step by step to accurate listening and pronunciation skills. It can be used equally as a self-study course, or in ESL (English as a Second Language) classrooms. The accent model we use is a modern, standard pronunciation called GB (General British) English.

Every drill and activity is accompanied by audio. Further tips for learners and teachers, and the most up to date information about training and materials to accompany the book, are available on our website thesoundofenglish.org.

Enjoy the course!

Joseph Hudson

Joseph Hudson

How to Use this Book

⊙

Audio

Download or stream the audio tracks at:
thesoundofenglish.org/audio/

Symbols

  ∩ 2.13   **Listen** (to recording 2.13)

  ⑉) 6.7   **Repeat** (after recording 6.7)

  ? 128   **Answers** (p. 128)

Diagrams

Vowel Sounds:
tongue, lip and jaw positions.

Consonant Sounds:
arrow shows place of articulation.

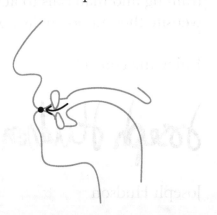

Chapters

This course contains 9 chapters. All learners should start with the Introduction Chapter (p. 2-12) to become familiar with the key concepts, terms, diagrams and sounds. Chapters 1-4 cover vowel sounds, Chapters 5-8 cover consonant sounds. These can be followed in the order they appear, or in a different order chosen by the learner or teacher.

Sections

Each chapter contains a combination of these sections:

SOUNDS	How to pronounce sounds with examples, IPA symbols and diagrams.
Spellings	How to choose the correct sounds based on their spellings.
Linking	How to join sounds and words together.
Activities	Sound selection, collocation, IPA and practice exercises.
sounds in accents	Features and variations in regional English accents.

Minimal Pairs

At the back of the book (pp. 110-117) the Minimal Pairs section covers 28 commonly confused sound pairs such as 'fit/feet' and 'ram /lamb'. The full list of sound pairs is found on p. 109.

Sound Chart

IPA symbols for each sound of English.

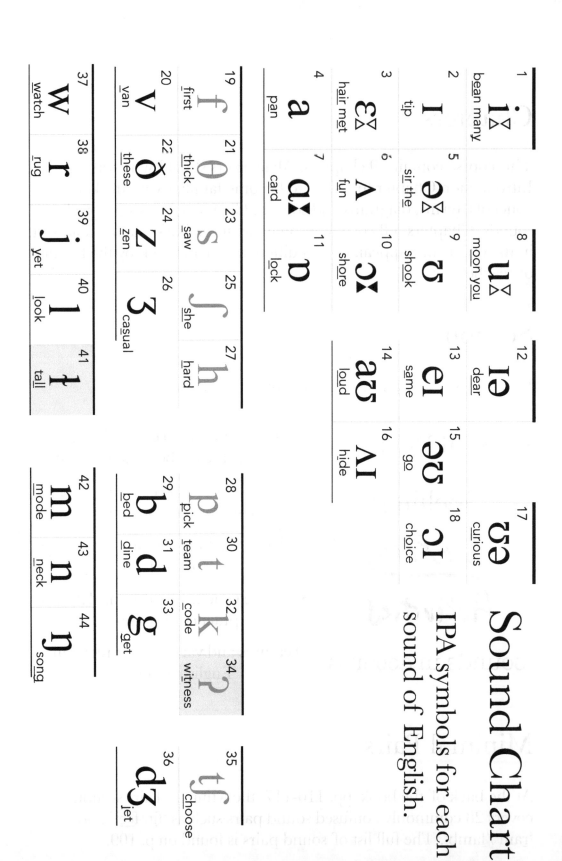

1 i̠ː bean ma̠ny	**8** uː mo̠on yo̠u
2 I tḭp	**12** Iə dear
3 ɛ̠ː ha̠ir me̠t	**17** ʊə cu̠rious
4 a pạn	
5 əː si̠r the̠	**9** ʊ shoo̠k
6 ʌ fụn	**13** eI sa̠me
7 ɑː ca̠rd	**15** əʊ go̠
10 ɔː sho̠re	**18** ɔI cho̠ice
11 ɒ lo̠ck	**14** aʊ lo̠ud
	16 ʌI hide
19 f fi̠rst	**28** p pi̠ck
20 v va̠n	**29** b be̠d
21 θ thi̠ck	**30** t te̠am
22 ð the̠se	**31** d di̠ne
23 s sa̠w	**32** k co̠de
24 z ze̠n	**33** g ge̠t
25 ʃ she̠	**34** ʔ wi̠tness
26 ʒ ca̠sual	**35** tʃ cho̠ose
27 h ha̠rd	**36** dʒ je̠t
37 w wa̠tch	**42** m mo̠de
38 r ru̠g	**43** n ne̠ck
39 j ye̠t	**44** ŋ so̠ng
40 l lo̠ok	
41 ɫ ta̠ll	

Sound Chart Key

See Introduction Chapter (pp. 2-12) for examples of each sound and practical explanations of all terms.

1-18   Vowel Sounds
19-44 Consonant Sounds

Vowel sound with long and short versions.

Long vowel sound.

t   Voiceless sound.

d   Voiced sound.

ʔ   Variation of a sound.

Transctiption Marks

/ /   IPA transcription e.g. /pɑːt/
/ ' /   Main stress in IPA transcription e.g. /ˈpɑːtnə/
< >   Written English e.g. < partner >
[ ]   Phonetic transcription (includes sound variations) e.g. [ʔ]

Version

The IPA symbols we use are the same as those found in the OED (Oxford English Dictionary). Other British English dictionaries may have slight variations. For examples of alternative IPA charts, visit thesoundofenglish.org/IPA/.

Vowel Sounds

⊙

Consonant Sounds |

◉

Θ

Made at Pronunciation Studio

Introduction

Vowel Sounds
are made by shaping air as it leaves the body.
Consonant Sounds
are made by blocking air as it leaves the body.

/baʊt/

h

1

Vowel Sounds

))) 0.1

Front Vowel Sounds / tongue towards front

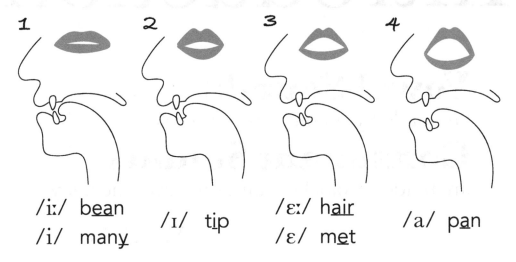

/iː/ bean
/i/ many

/ɪ/ tip

/ɛː/ hair
/ɛ/ met

/a/ pan

Central Vowel Sounds / tongue relatively flat

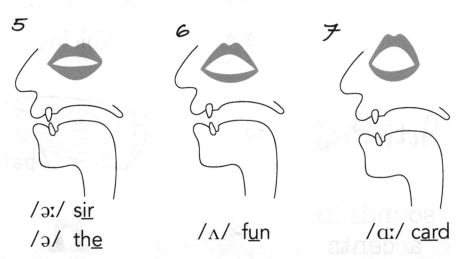

/əː/ sir
/ə/ the

/ʌ/ fun

/ɑː/ card

8-11. **Back Vowel Sounds** / tongue towards back

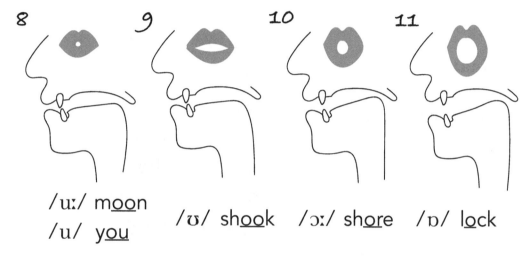

8   9   10   11

/uː/ m<u>oo</u>n
/u/ y<u>ou</u>

/ʊ/ sh<u>oo</u>k   /ɔː/ sh<u>ore</u>   /ɒ/ l<u>o</u>ck

12-18 **Diphthong Vowel Sounds**
/ move from one mouth position to another

12 /ɪə/ d<u>ear</u>

13 /eɪ/ s<u>a</u>me

14 /aʊ/ l<u>ou</u>d

15 /əʊ/ g<u>o</u>

16 /ʌɪ/ h<u>i</u>de

17 /ʊə/ c<u>u</u>rious

18 /ɔɪ/ ch<u>oi</u>ce

/hʌɪd/

Consonant Sounds

))) 0.2

Fricatives
made by squeezing air
through a small gap

19 /f/ first
20 /v/ van
21 /θ/ thick
22 /ð/ these
23 /s/ saw
24 /z/ zen
25 /ʃ/ she
26 /ʒ/ casual
27 /h/ hard

Plosives
made by fully blocking the
air as it leaves the body

28 /p/ pick
29 /b/ bed
30 /t/ team
31 /d/ dine
32 /k/ code
33 /g/ get
34 [ʔ] witness

Affricates
plosive directly followed by a fricative

35 /tʃ/ <u>ch</u>oose

36 /dʒ/ <u>j</u>et

Approximants
smooth vowel-like sounds made without contact

37 /w/ <u>w</u>atch

38 /r/ <u>r</u>ug

39 /j/ <u>y</u>et

Lateral Approximants
released through the sides of the tongue

40 /l/ <u>l</u>ook

41 [ɫ] ta<u>ll</u>

Nasals
made by releasing sound through the nose

42 /m/ <u>m</u>ode

43 /n/ <u>n</u>eck

44 /ŋ/ so<u>ng</u>

Consonant Articulation

- What is the difference in the pronunciation of the three sounds?

♩ 0.3
? 120

/p/ /t/ /k/

---------- ☉ ----------

Consonant sounds are made by **blocking air as it leaves the body**.
We use a range of places in the mouth and throat to block the air: **places of articulation**.

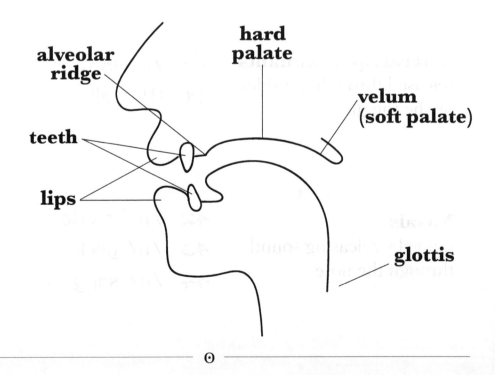

---------- ☉ ----------

🎧 0.4 – *Listen and match the places of articulation to their sounds:*

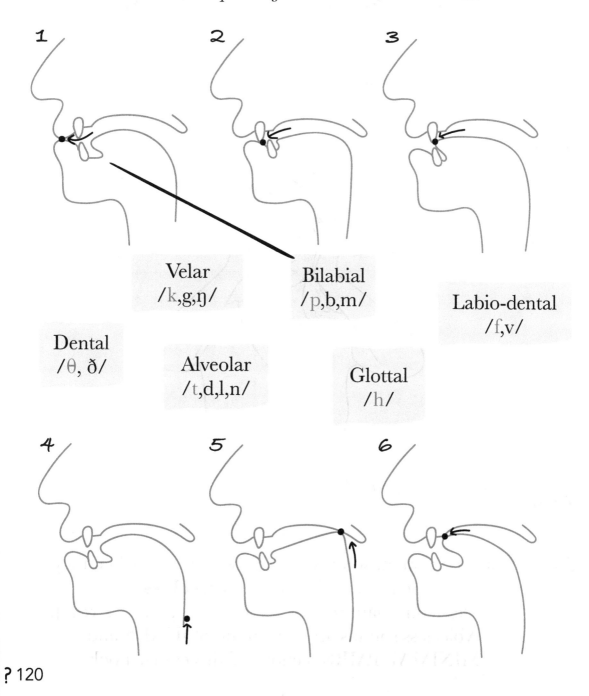

1

2

3

Velar
/k,g,ŋ/

Bilabial
/p,b,m/

Labio-dental
/f,v/

Dental
/θ, ð/

Alveolar
/t,d,l,n/

Glottal
/h/

4

5

6

? 120

Consonant Voicing

- Cover your ears with your hands and say the following sounds:

))) 0.5

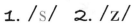

1. /s/   2. /z/

- What is the difference?

? 120

---⊙---

∩ 0.6   Some consonant sounds do not use the voice when they
are produced - they are **voiceless**.
Voiceless consonant sounds are /f,θ,s,ʃ,h,p,t,k,tʃ/ & [ʔ].
Voiceless sounds are grey in the SOUNDS and
MINIMAL PAIRS sections of this course book.

---⊙---

- *What is the difference in the pronunciation of the underlined sound?*

∩ 0.7

 cheese mouse

? 120

─────────────── ☉ ───────────────

It is not always possible to tell whether a sound is
voiced or voiceless from its spelling.

─────────────── ☉ ───────────────

- *Listen and decide which of the 2 words on the right, contains the
voiced consonant sound.*

		Voiced	Voiceless	Words
∩ 0.8	1	/d/	/t/	played placed
	2	/v/	/f/	off of
	3	/ð/	/θ/	author father
	4	/ʒ/	/ʃ/	mission vision
	5	/b/	/p/	bath path
	6	/dʒ/	/tʃ/	rich ridge
	7	/z/	/s/	business biscuit
	8	/g/	/k/	anger anchor

? 121

Activities

- *Listen and decide which word has a different vowel sound in each line:*

0.9

1. wool shook (cool) pull
2. put hut love flood
3. work north shirt burn
4. boat both broker bother
5. pair where earn pear
6. brown grow slow no
7. ear bare swear air
8. include wanted college taken
9. polite protect promise parade
10. calm aren't war heart
11. not watch cough tough

/bəʊt/

/hɑːt/

? 121

- *Match the words with their transcriptions.*

1	foreign	/ˈkʌbəd/
2	climb	/ˈfɒrɪn/
3	wrist	/hɑːf/
4	knot	/ˈɔːtəm/
5	half	/rɪst/
6	autumn	/klʌɪm/
7	listen	/θɔːt/
8	thought	/nɒt/
9	march	/ˈlɪs(ə)n/
10	cupboard	/mɑːtʃ/

? 121))) 0.10

- *Which silent consonant(s) does each word contain?*

1 __g__   2 ____   3 ____   4 ____   5 ____

6 ____   7 ____   8 ____   9 ____   10 ____

? 122

11

🎧 0.11   Moving just 50 miles in any direction in the British Isles normally results in significant changes in the local people's pronunciation. In this section of every chapter, we explore some of the most noticeable variations.

h

🎧 0.12

In the West Country, the locals never pronounce < h > so we say HOUSE, HAPPY, HEART (so that sounds the same as ART). This is known as 'h dropping' and it's found in many regions of England and Wales.

- Listen and decide if the accent is GB or West Country (WC):

🎧 0.13

1. I'm hungry, let's have some hot soup.   GB   WC

2. How heavy is that hammer?   GB   WC

3. Harry's on holiday in New Haven.   GB   WC

4. Have you heard of Henry Higgins?   GB   WC

5. Here's hoping the hotel's open!   GB   WC

❓122 **6.** My hair looks horrible, where's my hat?   GB   WC

Weak Vowels

are found in unstressed syllables of words and sentences.

ə

Spellings	Examples	Position
a	**a**gain sof**a**	Mid Jaw Centre Tongue Unrounded Lips
e	p**e**rsuade corn**e**r	
o	**o**bey oni**o**n	
u	s**u**ccess maxim**u**m	

))) 1.2 The German actor's second performance was sublime.
Listen to the thunder, the weather's horrendous tonight.

⊙

Schwa Spelling

- What do the underlined sounds have in common?

🎧 1.3

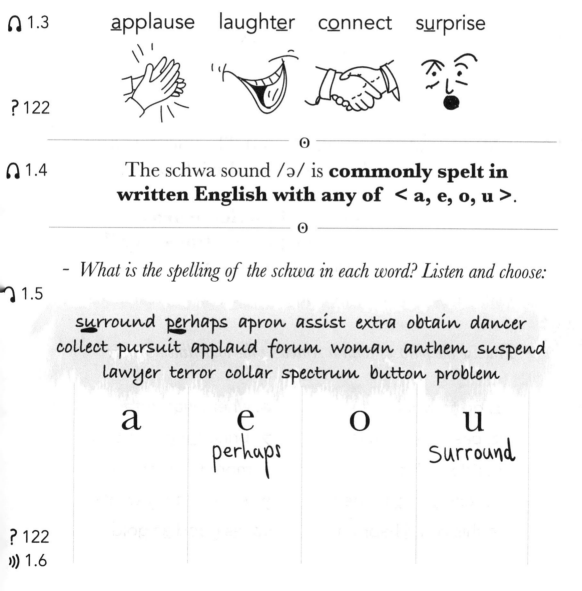

<u>a</u>pplause laught<u>e</u>r c<u>o</u>nnect s<u>u</u>rprise

? 122

⊙

🎧 1.4

The schwa sound /ə/ is **commonly spelt in written English with any of < a, e, o, u >**.

⊙

- What is the spelling of the schwa in each word? Listen and choose:

🎧 1.5

s<u>u</u>rround p<u>e</u>rhaps apron assist extra obtain dancer
collect pursuit applaud forum woman anthem suspend
lawyer terror collar spectrum button problem

a	e	o	u
	perhaps		surround

? 122
))) 1.6

15

Schwa Function Words

- Find two schwa sounds in the following sentence:

🎧 1.7

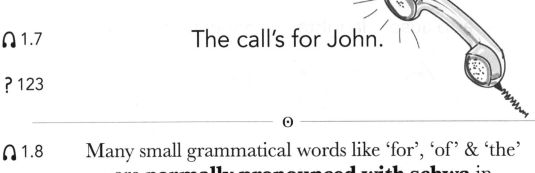

The call's for John.

? 123

---⊙---

🎧 1.8   Many small grammatical words like 'for', 'of' & 'the'
are **normally pronounced with schwa** in
connected speech.
These words are **function words**.
Many function words are **prepositions**, **auxiliary
verbs**, **pronouns**, **conjunctions** & **articles**.

---⊙---

- Practise the phrases with a schwa in the underlined words:

))) 1.9

1. go <u>to</u> work
2. pass <u>the</u> biscuits
3. ride <u>a</u> bike
4. send <u>some</u> money
5. this <u>could</u> happen

6. where <u>was</u> Peter
7. bring <u>them</u> back
8. more <u>than</u> three
9. what <u>do</u> they want
10. <u>as</u> good <u>as</u> gold

– Complete the sentences with a word below:

> her   than   some   can   to
> from   your   should   are   the

1. _____ we go now?

2. It's more _____ 30 degrees outside!

3. Let's go _____ Thailand this summer.

4. I met _____ Smiths last night.

5. Why _____ you looking at me like that?

6. We _____ meet up soon.

7. I'd like _____ more coffee please.

8. Is that _____ wedding ring?

9. _____ first husband is a designer.

10. He's originally _____ Greece.

? 123
))) 1.10

– Create your own sentences with the words below:

> of   does   them   was   must   just

Weak vs Strong

- Compare the pronunciations of the word 'from' in this dialogue:

∩1.11   A Where are you <u>from</u>?

       B I'm <u>from</u> London.

? 123

---------------------------------⊙---------------------------------

∩1.12   Many **function words have 2 pronunciations**:

<u>i) **a weak form:**</u>
in connected speech
(I'm from London. /frəm/).

<u>ii) **a strong form:**</u>
when **at the end** of a unit/sentence
(Where are you from? /frɒm/).

when **emphasised**
(Is it really *from* the palace? /frɒm/).

when said **in isolation**.
(From. /frɒm/).

---------------------------------⊙---------------------------------

- Decide if the underlined word is in its weak or strong form.

🎧 1.13

1 A Can we go to the shops now?   weak
   B You can. I'm staying in.   strong

2 A I don't know who these clothes are for.
   B They're not for me.

3 A That is some building.
   B Yes, it needs some work on the roof though.

4 A Your shirt's dirty!
   B Well your trousers are torn.

5 A Shall we go to the cinema?
   B I don't really want to.

6 A Ask them if they'd like to join us.
   B Them? No way.

7 A What are you doing?
   B Are you sure you want to know?

8 A Look, I've got money and nice clothes.
   B And? I'm not going to go out with you.

? 123))) 1.14

19

ɪ i u

⊙

Schwa is not the only weak vowel sound in English.
The sounds **/ɪ,i,u/ also appear on weak syllables**.

))) 1.15

Weak Function Words	Weak Syllables
Only before a consonant sound.	
< i >	< i, e, a>
ɪ if in it is him his this will	**i**nvolve someth**i**ng walk**i**ng **e**njoy b**e**lieve bask**e**t man**a**ge or**a**nge
Only at the end of a word or root word.	
< e >	< y, ie, ey, e, i >
i m**e** sh**e** w**e** b**e** th**e**	ver**y** an**y** slowl**y** fish**y** happ**y** dodg**y** bab**ie**s donk**ey** recip**e** bikin**i**
< ou, o >	
u y**ou** wh**o** t**o** d**o**	

⊙

20

– Place the words in the columns according to the underlined sound:

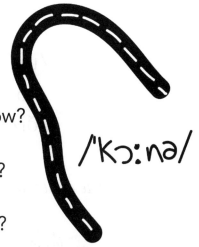

🎧 1.16

cosy   cottage   cotton   shaker   shaking
shaky   really   release   surreal   evolve   volley
evolution   woman   women   womanly

/ɪ/	/i/	/ə/
	cosy	

? 123   ))) 1.17

– Choose each underlined weak vowel sound using only /ə,ɪ,i,u/:

🎧 1.18

1. Did you enjoy the show?
    I   u ɪ   ə

2. Can it corner quickly?

3. Will he manage to see them now?

4. Are we going to do something?

/ˈkɔːnə/

5. You said it was already finished?

? 124

21

to & the

- How many pronunciations of 'to' and 'the' do you hear below?

∩ 1.19   to Brazil   to Argentina

             the Nigerian   the Egyptian

? 124

⊙

∩ 1.20   The weak function words 'to' and 'the' **change pronunciation before vowel sounds** as follows:

'to': **/tə/** changes to **/tu/**.

'the': **/ðə/** changes to **/ði/**.

⊙

))) 1.21   /tə/   drink hate close seek

          /tu/   eat enjoy open avoid

          /ðə/   water calm banana start

          /ði/   air angry apple end

- Create combinations with 'to' & 'the' and the words below:

> drive   interest   bank   open
> time   empty   space   orbit

∩ 1.22

Schwa Linking

- How does the first word join to the next in each combination?

🎧 1.23   theatre entrance   drama award

❓ 124

ʘ

🎧 1.24   In connected speech, **the schwa sound links to a following vowel sound with /r/.**
This occurs **even when no < r > is found in the spelling**, which is known as '**intrusive r**'.

ʘ

- Match the first word to the next that you hear:

🎧 1.25

/ˈkɒmə/

1. harbour   aerobics
2. sofa   outfit
3. water   entrance
4. comma   after 'and'
5. circular   orbit
6. fauna   of love
7. sailor   outlet
8. labour   and flora

- Practise the combinations linking with /r/.

sounds in accents

i

🎧 1.26 In Birmingham and throughout the West Midlands of England, the local accents make the final weak /i/ sound into /eɪ/ so we say LOVEL<u>Y</u>, FANC<u>Y</u>, BUNN<u>Y</u>.

- Listen and decide if the accent is GB or regional:

🎧 1.27 **1.** This is a lovely symphony.   GB   Regional

2. I'm hungry, actually.   GB   Regional

3. We're usually a bit silly.   GB   Regional

4. It will be partly cloudy.   GB   Regional

5. Jonny, you're early!   GB   Regional

6. An unlikely story.   GB   Regional

7. Basically, I'm really lonely.   GB   Regional

8. That film is seriously funny.   GB   Regional

? 124

2

Short Vowels

25

I

))) 2.1

Spellings	Examples	Position
i e y	**p**i**t** **si**n **ri**nse **i**njure **E**ngland pr**e**tty s**y**stem rh**y**thm	Close-mid Jaw Near-front Tongue Slightly Spread Lips

))) 2.2

Sit still and think quickly.
Little things can fit in the wings.

ʊ

⊙

Spellings	Examples	Position
u	put full bush	Close-mid Jaw Slightly Back Tongue Unrounded Lips 
oo	good look wool	
o	woman	
ou	should	

))) 2.4

Look at the butcher's book, it's full of wool.
We took wood and sugar to the cook.

⊙

ɛ

Spellings	Examples	Position
e	**s**e**nd**	Mid Jaw Front Tongue Unrounded Lips
	b**et**	
	sh**ell**	
ea	dr**ea**d	
	h**ea**d	
	d**ea**th	
a	**a**ny	
	m**a**ny	

Let's send our friends some bread.
Were you fed any healthy hen eggs?

28

ʌ

Spellings	Examples	Position
u o ou oo	sum bun shut love money son rough blood	Mid-open Jaw Centre Tongue Unrounded Lips 

))) 2.8 It's wonderful fun, then Monday comes.
This country must encourage its young.

ɒ

))) 2.9

Spellings	Examples	Position
o a au ou	p**o**t b**o**g l**o**dge w**a**sh qu**a**lity bec**au**se s**au**sage c**ou**gh	Open Jaw Back Tongue Rounded Lips

))) 2.10

What a lot of nonsense, Robert.
Honestly, I'm sorry the watch stopped.

a

))) 2.11

Spellings	Examples	Position
a	sand ham pack badge rap latch angry attic	Open Jaw Front Tongue Unrounded Lips

))) 2.12

That's fantastic Sam, thanks.
Hand the backgammon pack to Fran.

⊙

31

short vowel Activities

– Put the words into the boxes according to their vowel sounds:

enough   health   fist   gone   land   shook
watch   back   symbol   none   splash   sell
push   hot   bend   English   ant   sun
quarrel   could   ship   rush   breath   stood

I	ʊ	ɛ

ɒ	ʌ	a
	enough	

- *Write the words (they have unusual spellings):*

1. /ˈwɪmɪn/ **Women**
2. /wʌns/
3. /əˈgɛn/
4. /ˈbɪznɪs/
5. /ˈsɛz/

6. /ˈdʌz/
7. /ˈfrend/
8. /ˈbɪlt/
9. /ˈflʌd/
10. /ˈsɒsɪdʒ/

? 125))) 2.15

- *Make 2 common words by placing different short vowel sounds in the gaps:*

1) /l__v/
   /ɪ/ **live**
   /ʌ/ **love**

2) /b__d/

3) /θ__ŋk/

4) /ʃ__d/

5) /w__tʃ/

6) /f__l/

7) /s__ŋ/

8) /ʃ__p/

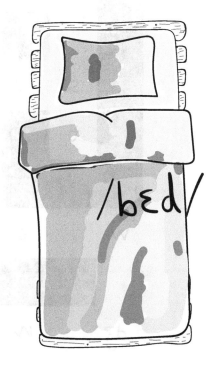
/bɛd/

? 125))) 2.16

CROSSWORD

- *Complete the IPA crossword using the clues on the next page and only the vowel sounds below:*

ɪ ʊ ɛ ʌ ɒ a i ə

DOWN

1. Verb, opposite of /pʊl/.

2. Chart showing days, /mʌnθs/ and weeks.

3. The price of something, often in /ˈmʌni/.

5. To /mɪks/ different things together.

7. A serious, immoral /akt/.

9. Adjective, something /ˈkɒmɪk(ə)l/ causing laughter.

10. A triangular /blɒk/ or shape of material or cheese.

ACROSS

2. /sɒft/ bag of material to make chairs comfortable.

3. A violent /ˌkɒnfrʌnˈteɪʃn/ or mismatch.

4. A person who steals, possibly from a /baŋk/.

6. Movement from one side to the /ˈʌðə/.

7. Past /tɛns/ of 'say'.

8. /ˈfrɛnli/ whale known for jumping.

10. Man with /ˈmadʒɪk(ə)l/ powers.

11. Directly below, /ˈɒpəzɪt/ of above.

12. First month of the year, after /dɪˈsɛmbə/.

? 126 ∩ 2.17

35

sounds in accents

Λ

🎧 2.18

In Yorkshire, the local people don't ever use the /ʌ/ vowel sound, we replace it with /ʊ/: FUN, LOVE, ROUGH, so for us LOOK and LUCK sound the same. This happens in most regional accents in the North and Midlands of England.

- Listen and decide if the accent is GB or regional:

🎧 2.19

1. Enough's enough, son.   GB   Regional

2. I should have done something.   GB   Regional

3. Unbelievable, we won the cup!   GB   Regional

4. Doug's coming up on Monday.   GB   Regional

5. Such wonderful sunshine!   GB   Regional

6. There's nothing underneath.   GB   Regional

7. I won roughly a hundred quid.   GB   Regional

8. It's been a lovely Sunday lunch. GB   Regional

? 126

3

Long Vowels

 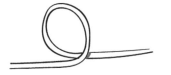

Spellings	Examples	Position
ee ea ei ie i e	meet seed each leap seize piece machine be	Close Jaw Front Tongue Spread Lips

))) 3.2   I need sleep and a decent meal.
Please eat your greens, Steven.

38

u

Spellings	Examples	Position
ew oo o ou ue ui	n**ew** gr**ew** b**oo**t f**oo**d l**o**se s**ou**p gl**ue** s**ui**t	Close Jaw Near-back Tongue Rounded Lips

))) 3.4

You kn**ew** wh**o** dr**ew** it bl**ue**?
S**oo**n I'll ch**oo**se my s**ui**t for the d**ue**t.

39

əː

))) 3.5

Spellings	Examples	Position
ir ur er (w)or ear our	sh**ir**t b**ir**d t**ur**n c**ur**l s**er**vant w**or**ld h**ear**d j**our**ney	Mid Jaw Centre Tongue Unrounded Lips 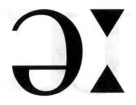

))) 3.6

F**ir**stly, it's w**or**th l**ear**ning the w**or**ds.
But s**ir**, I h**ear**d you w**er**en't ret**ur**ning.

Spellings	Examples	Position
al aw or our oor ure ou	t**al**k s**aw** r**aw** sh**or**t f**our** p**oor** s**ur**e b**ou**ght	Mid Jaw Back Tongue Rounded Lips

So**r**t the b**al**ls in **or**der of imp**or**tance.
Div**or**ce **law** is **al**ways a ch**or**e.

Ɛⱽ

Spellings	Examples	Position
ar	sh**ar**e aw**ar**e v**ar**ious sc**ar**ce	Open-mid Jaw Front Tongue Unrounded Lips
air	**air** aff**air**	
ear ae	sw**ear** **ae**rial	

))) 3.10 I sw**ear** the p**ar**ents c**ar**ed for th**eir** welf**ar**e.
Wh**er**e's the f**air** h**air**ed m**ar**e?

ɑː

Spellings	Examples	Position
ar	**d**a**r**k **far**m **b**a**r**	Open Jaw Centre Tongue Unrounded Lips
a	gl**a**ss p**a**ss f**a**st	
al	c**al**m p**al**m	

))) 3.12

It can't harm to laugh harder.
Aren't you on after Lance's father?

43

Long vowel Activities

- *Place the words in the columns according to their vowel sounds:*

🎧 3.13 half search reach flare soon lawn worth fruit
shark move door chair drew charm fa<u>iry</u>
sheet hurt sought eve <u>jour</u>nal bath tore niece
first fall scene wear route hard v<u>ary</u>

iː	uː	ɜː

ɔː	ɛː	ɑː
		half

- *Write the words in English:*

1. /bɔːn/   __born__   2. /tiːm/   _____

3. /luːp/   _____   4. /fɛː/   _____

5. /wəːk/   _____   6. /truː/   _____

7. /fɑː/   _____   8. /hɑːd/   _____

9. /səː/   _____   10. /niː/   _____

11. /rɔː/   _____   12. /skwɛː/   _____

? 127))) 3.15

- *Complete the proverbs with a word from the previous exercise:*

1. All __work__ and no play makes Jack a dull boy.

2. He's as _____ as nails.

3. I got the ____ end of the deal.

4. We're ____ deep in trouble.

5. Can you keep me in the ____.

6. I won that game _____ and _____.

/luːp/

? 127))) 3.16

45

Reduced Vowel Length

- *Listen and decide which word contains the shortest /iː/ sound:*

⋒ 3.17   bee   beach   bead

? 128

-- ☉ --

⋒ 3.18   Long vowel sounds are **shortened if the
following sound is a voiceless consonant**
/p,t,k,f,θ,s,ʃ,tʃ/.
These are known as **reduced vowels**.

-- ☉ --

))) 3.19   *full length*   *reduced*

	full length	reduced
/iː/	seed	seat
/uː/	prove	proof
/əː/	fur	first
/ɑː/	large	lark
/ɔː/	corn	cork

46

- Circle the word containing a reduced vowel in each group:

1. lead leave (leaf)
2. fought ford four
3. sir surf surge
4. boot boo boom
5. peace pee peas
6. hard halve half
7. tour torch tall
8. occ<u>ur</u> conc<u>ern</u> ins<u>ert</u>
9. farm farce far
10. tooth two tomb

/liːf/

? 128))) 3.20

- Fill in the gaps in the chart below:

	word (full length)	+ /d/ (full length)	+ /t/ (reduced)
/bɔː/	bore		bought
/hɜː/		heard/herd	
/kɑː/	car		
/niː/		need	
/suː/			

? 128))) 3.21

47

sounds in accents

ɑː

🎧 3.22

In Scottish accents of English, there are lots of words spelt with < a > like CH<u>A</u>NCE, B<u>A</u>TH, GL<u>A</u>SS that are made with /a/ not /ɑː/. Nearly all American and Northern English accents also pronounce these words with /a/.

- All the words below would be pronounced /ɑː/ in GB English. Circle those that you hear pronounced with /a/.

🎧 3.23   **aunt   can't   disaster   master**

gasp   path   laugh   clasp

advance   France   glance   chance

example   sample   fast   last

ask   task   pass   grass

❓ 128

48

4

Diphthongs
are long vowel sounds made by moving from one position of the mouth to another.

SOUNDS	50-55	ɪə eɪ aʊ əʊ ʌɪ ɔɪ
	56-57	ʊə
Activities	58-59	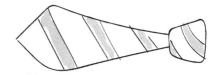
sounds in accents	60	**əʊ**

ɪə

Spellings	Examples	Position 1	Position 2
er ear eer ea eu eo i	p**er**iod h**ere** **ear** ch**eer** Kor**ea**n mus**eu**m th**eo**ry del**i**rious	Close-mid Near-front Unrounded	Mid Centre Unrounded

Year ze**ro** is n**ear**, we f**ear**.
Since**re**ly, it's cl**ear** my id**ea** of a h**er**o is not h**er**e.

eɪ

Spellings	Examples	Position 1	Position 2
		Mid Front Unrounded	Close-mid Near-front Unrounded
a	pace came		
ai	gain fail		
ay	bay spray		
ei ea	eight steak		

They say fame's a dangerous game.
Waiter, take these plates away.

aʊ

))) 4.5

Spellings	Examples	Position 1	Position 2
ou ow	**ou**t p**ou**nd m**ou**th r**ou**nd n**ow** t**ow**er p**ow**der cl**ow**n	Open Centre Unrounded	Close-mid Slightly Back Rounded

))) 4.6

In **tow**n the cr**ow**ds s**ou**nd l**ou**der.
I d**ou**bt the c**ou**ncil will all**ow** the h**ou**sing.

⊙

52

əʊ

))) 4.7

Spellings	Examples	Position 1	Position 2
		Open-mid Centre Unrounded	Close-mid Slightly Back Rounded
o	b**o**ne		
	v**o**te		
	n**o**		
	p**o**ny		
oe	t**oe**		
ow	l**ow**		
oa	**oa**k		
ou	th**ou**gh		

))) 4.8   N**o**, d**o**n't m**oa**n **o**ver the ph**o**ne.
Alth**ou**gh the r**oa**d is s**oa**ked, he'll g**o**.

⊙

53

ΛI

Spellings	Examples	Position 1	Position 2
i ie ei y	p**i**ne d**i**ce h**i**gh m**i**ght l**ie** tr**ie**d **ei**ther wh**y**	Open Centre Unrounded	Close-mid Near-front Unrounded

))) 4.10   Fine wine and light bites tonight.
I dislike high and mighty types.

ɔɪ

))) 4.11

Spellings	Examples	Position 1	Position 2
oi oy	**oi**l p**oi**nt v**oi**d v**oi**ce j**oi**n b**oy** v**oy**age empl**oy**	Open-mid Back Rounded	Close-mid Near-front Unrounded

))) 4.12

The ann**oy**ing n**oi**ses sp**oi**lt the b**oy**'s j**oy**.
My ch**oi**ce as empl**oy**er is to app**oi**t Fl**oy**d.

ʊə

))) 4.13

Spellings	Examples	Position 1	Position 2
ur oor our	p**ur**e s**ur**ely d**ur**ing f**ur**y pl**ur**al p**oor** m**oor** t**our**	Close-mid Slightly Back Unrounded	Mid Centre Unrounded

))) 4.14   Sec**ur**ity d**ur**ing the t**our**nament was p**oor**.
The pl**ur**al of **tour** is s**ur**ely '**tour**s'.

56

- Listen to the following words said 3 ways, what's the difference?

🎧 4.15
❓ 129

<u>su</u>re d<u>u</u>ring p<u>oo</u>r

🎧 4.16 The diphthong **/ʊə/ is often replaced** with long single (monophthong) vowel sounds in GB English. The 2 alternatives are **long sound /ɔː/** (p. 41), or a **long version of short sound /ʊ/** (p. 27).

- Listen and place the words in the columns according to the alternative pronunciation you hear of /ʊə/:

🎧 4.17

cur<u>i</u>ous   sure   pl<u>ur</u>al   tour   moor   s<u>u</u>rely
d<u>u</u>ring   pure   poor   p<u>ue</u>rile   f<u>u</u>rious   dem<u>u</u>re

/ɔː/	long /ʊ/
	cur<u>i</u>ous

❓ 129))) 4.18

57

diphthong Activities

- Put the words into the boxes according to their vowel sounds:

♫ 4.19

foam boil ab<u>ou</u>t tape height beer cra<u>y</u>on
tried mat<u>e</u>rial toy joke vow aim expl<u>o</u>sion
loud asylum lo<u>y</u>al year pill<u>ow</u> choice
bike break p<u>ow</u>er sinc<u>e</u>re

eɪ	ɔɪ	ʌɪ

əʊ	aʊ	ɪə
foam		

- Add diphthongs to the gaps to make 2 or more words:

/taɪ/

1. b__t /eɪ/ bait
2. n__
3. fl__
4. pl__
5. sp__
6. dr__n
7. t__
8. m__n

? 130))) 4.21

- Each expression uses a diphthong twice, listen to the sentences and write the words and diphthong you hear for each:

eɪ ɔɪ ʌɪ ə̶ʊ̶ aʊ ɪə

ᛁ 4.22

1. "s_o__ s_o_" /əʊ/
2. "p___ d___"
3. "h___ h___"
4. "h___ t___me"
5. "___t and ___t"
6. "h___ty t___ty"

? 130))) 4.23

🎧 4.24

In and around Newcastle the /əʊ/ diphthong is pronounced [oə]: G<u>O</u>, SH<u>OW</u>, L<u>O</u>NELY. This accent's often referred to as 'Geordie'.

In Liverpool, lots of speakers pronounce it [ɛʊ]: G<u>O</u>, SH<u>OW</u>, L<u>O</u>NELY. The accent's known as 'Liverpudlian' or 'Scouse'.

- Listen to each sentence said three times and write the order you hear them:

🎧 4.25

	GB	Geordie	Scouse
A. No, I don't know.			
B. Row the boat, Tony.			
C. Both roads are slow.			
D. I'm so lonely on my own.			
E. Phone me at home, ok?			

? 130

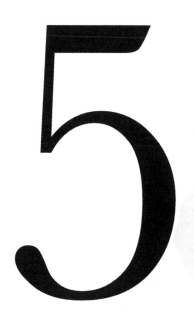

Fricatives

are made by squeezing air through
a small gap.

SOUNDS	62-66	f v θ ð s z ʃ ʒ h
Spellings	67	Silent < h >
	68-69	< s > Endings
Activities	70-71	
sounds in accents	72	**th**

f v

))) 5.1

Spellings / Examples	Position
< f, ph, gh >	
f far **f**inish **f**ree loa**f** aw**f**ul bu**ff**er **ph**one gra**ph** lau**gh**ter enou**gh**	
< v, f >	
v **v**ain **v**ote **v**alue in**v**ol**v**e se**v**ere **v**iew lo**v**e lea**v**e e**v**en o**f**	

))) 5.2

Fight for values, live for laughter.
Have you phoned all of Vincent's friends?

62

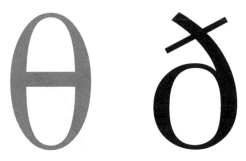

θ

Spellings / Examples	Position
< th >	
θ thank thin thought thumb three bath cloth maths health length	
< th >	
ð the those them though father neither Northern bathe soothe clothes	

I think the path is further than that.
This is neither the North nor the South.

θ

S Z

Spellings / Examples	Position
< s, c, sc >	
S see so sort fossil mass past face sauce mice science scene	
< s, z, x >	
Z lose chose cheese prison freeze scissor zoo zero fizz xylophone	

)) 5.6   This soup is losing its taste so let's sprinkle some salt. It's zero degrees, I'm freezing! Please start the heaters.

ʃ 3

○

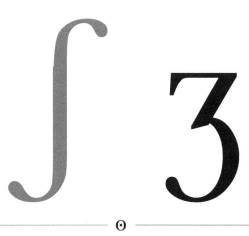

)) 5.7

Spellings / Examples	Position
< sh, ch, ss, su, c/sc/s/t+i >	
ʃ **sh**ark **sh**ine fi**sh** ma**ch**ine **ch**ef pa**ss**ion **su**re con**sc**ious man**s**ion spa**ti**al	
< ge, si, su, g >	
3 massa**ge** colla**ge** mira**ge** bei**ge** preci**si**on fu**si**on vi**si**on u**su**al mea**su**re **g**enre	

)) 5.8   Unfa**sh**ionable ca**su**al **sh**irts **su**rely **sh**ocked the re**g**ime. A**si**an fu**si**on **ch**efs are u**su**ally pa**ss**ionate about fi**sh**.

○

h

))) 5.9

Spellings / Examples	Position
< h >	
hand head hit who whole hair hawk ahead inhibit perhaps	

))) 5.10   Hundreds of horses' hooves hid the horrific hilltop.
His house happened to be inhabited by hungry hedgehogs.

Silent < h >

– *Complete the crossword using the clues below:*

/gəʊst/

1. Goodness or virtue.
2. A display or presentation.
3. The successor or next in line.
4. An automobile or channel.
5. A phantom or spirit.

6. The belly or abdomen.
7. Somebody who herds sheep.
8. Truthful or genuine.
9. To speak softly or murmur.
10. Extremely tired or fatigued.

131

5.11 – *Practise the words with silent* h .

fricative Activities

- *Listen and select the pronunciation of < th >:*

🎧 5.12

1. wor<u>th</u> (θ) ð
2. wea<u>th</u>er θ ð
3. four<u>th</u> θ ð
4. fur<u>th</u>er θ ð
5. <u>th</u>ese θ ð

6. <u>th</u>eory θ ð
7. pa<u>th</u> θ ð
8. pa<u>th</u>s θ ð
9. ba<u>th</u>e θ ð
10. ba<u>th</u> θ ð

? 131

- *Write the underlined fricative sound in IPA next to each word (use each sound once):*

f v θ ð s z ʃ ʒ h

<u>sh</u>ell ʃ   <u>th</u>ank __   lau<u>gh</u> __

pa<u>c</u>e __   ero<u>s</u>ion __   bo<u>th</u>er __

ra<u>v</u>e __   choo<u>s</u>e __   <u>h</u>ot __

? 131))) 5.13

68

- Match the IPA transcriptions with Word 1:

		IPA	Word 1	Word 2
	1	/nəʊz/	through	
	2	/sɔː/	hare	
	3	/pɔːz/	pause	
	4	/θruː/	seize	
	5	/ˈsteɪʃ(ə)n(ə)ri/	there	
	6	/hɛː/	shear	
	7	/ʃɪə/	nose	Knows
	8	/θrəʊn/	thrown	
	9	/siːz/	sore	
	10	/ðɛː/	stationery	

- Think of another word with identical pronunciation in 'Word 2'.

❓131 �))) 5.14

---------------------------------- ☉ ----------------------------------

♩5.15 Two or more words with the **same pronunciation and different spellings** are called **homophones**.

---------------------------------- ☉ ----------------------------------

< s > Endings

- How is < s > pronounced differently in these two words?

🎧 5.16

?132

locks   logs

---------------------------------- ☉ ----------------------------------

🎧 5.17 If you add < s > to a word, it is pronounced:
/z/ after a voiced sound (he's, hands, loves).
/s/ after a voiceless sound (it's, facts, rocks).

---------------------------------- ☉ ----------------------------------

🔊 5.18 **/ z /** rubs he's moves bathes roams
         bars pays loads rings ours

     / s / wraps hops it's tricks moths
         lamps that's shark's

– Add an <s> ending to the words and circle the correct pronunciation:

1. stick   /s/ /z/   6. that   /s/ /z/

2. stone   /s/ /z/   7. thing   /s/ /z/

3. slab   /s/ /z/   8. think   /s/ /z/

4. slap   /s/ /z/   9. know   /s/ /z/

5. their   /s/ /z/   10. laugh   /s/ /z/

? 132))) 5.19

⊙

∩ 5.20   An < es > or < s > ending **after /s, z, ʃ, ʒ, tʃ, dʒ/ is pronounced /ɪz/** (miss__es__, phas__es__, watch__es__, fudg__es__). This **can be written as a possessive** (bo__ss'__).

⊙

– Add an < s > or < es > ending to the words and pronounce them:

rose judge James ridge
mortgage bus rich miss
cheese fox hatch Jones
fuss raise cottage

/ˈbʌsɪz/

))) 5.21

sounds in accents

th

🎧 5.22

In London and many other urban regions of England, the local accents don't include /θ/ or /ð/, instead the 'th' sounds are normally pronounced /f/ and /v/: THANKS, THEATRE, BROTHER, WITH.

- Listen and decide if the accent is GB or regional:

🎧 5.23

1. I think so.   GB   Regional

2. That's pathetic.   GB   Regional

3. Think nothing of it.   GB   Regional

4. It's further than I thought.   GB   Regional

5. This is the seventh time.   GB   Regional

6. Thanks, that's so thoughtful!   GB   Regional

7. They're really thirsty.   GB   Regional

8. The thing is, he's my brother!   GB   Regional

❓ 132

6

Plosives
are made by fully blocking the air as it leaves the body.

Affricates
consist of a plosive directly followed by a fricative.

	74-76	p b t d k g
SOUNDS	77	tʃ dʒ
	78	?
	79	Silent Letters
Spellings	80-81	< t >
	82-83	< ed > Endings
sounds in accents	84	?

p b

))) 6.1

Spellings / Examples	Position
< p >	
p **p**eace **p**ark **p**ony **p**ie **p**rint a**pp**ly s**p**ray a**pp**le ram**p** cli**p**	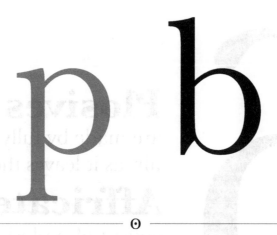
< b >	
b **b**oot **b**ored **b**ook **b**oat **b**reak **b**lame ro**bb**er fa**b**ulous lo**b** **b**ul**b**	

))) 6.2 Pick u**p** a **b**lue um**b**rella **b**efore de**p**arting.
Playing **p**iggy**b**acks at the **p**arty a**b**sor**b**ed the **b**oys completely.

74

t d

⊙

Spellings / Examples	Position
< t, ed >	
t **t**alk **t**en **t**oy **t**own **t**rick **t**wist **t**une wri**tt**en accen**t** wash**ed**	
< d, ed >	
d **d**ark **d**uck **d**og **d**ine **d**ry mi**dd**le su**dd**en re**d** swor**d** play**ed**	

⟩⟩ 6.4   Tonigh**t**, le**t**'s spen**d** some **t**ime **d**oing no**t** a lo**t** a**t** all.
Davi**d**'s **d**eb**t**s spiralle**d** ou**t** of con**t**rol un**t**il he sough**t** a**d**vice.

⊙
---

k g

Spellings / Examples	Position
< k, c, q, ch, ck, x >	
k — **k**it **c**ome **c**urse **ch**rome **q**uite **c**lown ban**k** a**cc**ount bla**ck** e**x**plain	
< g, x >	
g — **g**ive **g**one **g**ate **g**o **g**lad **g**rid be**gg**ar e**gg** **g**uide e**x**ist	

)) 6.6   Loo**k**, **q**uite a **g**ood e**x**ample of a blo**g** on **c**rime fi**c**tion.
Kate's **G**ree**k** **g**uests **c**ame ba**ck** **c**raving English **c**uisine.

tʃ dʒ

Spellings / Examples	Position
< ch, tch, ti, tu >	
tʃ **ch**eat **ch**at **ch**air a**ch**ieve por**ch** **c**ou**ch** stret**ch** wat**ch** sugges**ti**on ques**ti**on **tu**na	
< g, j, dg >	
dʒ **g**in **g**el **g**iant pi**g**eon **j**oke **j**ourney **j**oin ba**dg**er ri**dg**e lo**dg**e **j**u**dg**e	

This **j**am **j**ar is actually atta**ch**ed to the fri**dg**e.
Whi**ch** bu**tch**er su**gg**ested pi**g**eon for lun**ch**?

Spellings / Examples	Position
< t >	
cutback rightly fitness Britpop setback pothole gatepost witness outright nutmeg	

In a nutshell, not many cat flaps have white doors. Lightning isn't common in Hertfordshire or Wiltshire.

Silent Letters

- Match the pictures with their IPA transcriptions:

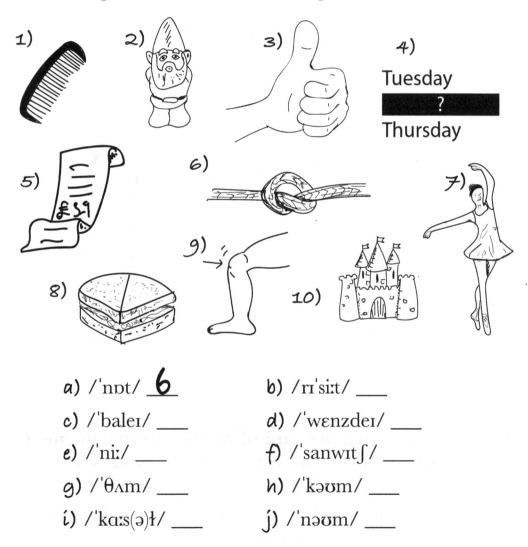

1)
2)
3)
4)
Tuesday
?
Thursday

5)
6)
7)

9)

8)
10)

a) /ˈnɒt/ **6**   b) /rɪˈsiːt/ ___

c) /ˈbaleɪ/ ___   d) /ˈwɛnzdeɪ/ ___

e) /ˈniː/ ___   f) /ˈsanwɪtʃ/ ___

g) /ˈθʌm/ ___   h) /ˈkəʊm/ ___

i) /ˈkɑːs(ə)ɫ/ ___   j) /ˈnəʊm/ ___

- Which letter is silent in each word?

? 132))) 6.11

< t >

– *Which < t > is pronounced differently?*

🎧 6.12

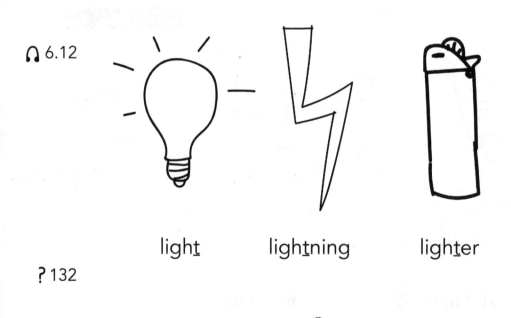

light lightning lighter

? 132

⊙

🎧 6.13 When /t/ is at the **end of a syllable** and the **next sound is a consonant**, /t/ can be pronounced [ʔ] in fast connected speech.

This occurs within words (ligh<u>t</u>ning) and between words (i<u>t</u> was).

⊙

– Practise the word pairs using [ʔ] in the second (underlined) < t >:

t

bat / ba<u>t</u>man

late / la<u>t</u>ely

pot / po<u>t</u>hole

fit / fi<u>t</u>ness

hat / ha<u>t</u>stand

bit / bi<u>t</u>coin

?

– Which < t > could be pronounced [ʔ] in each sentence?

1. I<u>t</u> was true!

2. Time to get back!

3. What type of cat is it?

4. Can't I sit here?

5. Talk about wasting water!

6. Absolutely not!

/Kat/

< ed > Endings

∩ 6.16   stopp<u>ed</u>   paus<u>ed</u>   start<u>ed</u>   finish<u>ed</u>

? 133

∩ 6.17   <ed> endings are pronounced:

/d/ after a voiced sound (play<u>ed</u>, judg<u>ed</u>).

/t/ after a voiceless sound (finish<u>ed</u>, watch<u>ed</u>).

/ɪd/ after /t/ or /d/ (want<u>ed</u>, fad<u>ed</u>).

))) 6.18   /d/   rubbed logged moved bathed
                     phased fudged roamed barred

            /t/   wrapped hopped locked tricked
                     missed washed fetched laughed

            /ɪd/   rated looted painted started
                     loaded needed jaded eroded

- Add < ed > to these words and place them in the correct column:

6.19 pour afford shop rip boast raid bail mess boo
fish bloat wash sew please fetch need cart
arrange lick herd loan rob trek allude

/t/	/d/	/ɪd/
	poured	

? 133))) 6.20

⊙

6.21 **Some adjectives** ending with < ed > are
pronounced with **/ɪd/ regardless of the sound
before the ending** (crook<u>ed</u>, rugg<u>ed</u>).

⊙

- Write the word ending < ed > in each sentence you hear below:

6.22 1. dogged 2. _____ 3. _____ 4. _____

5. _____ 6. _____ 7. _____ 8. _____

? 133))) 6.23

83

sounds in accents

?

🎧 6.24

In Manchester and in most areas of Britain, local people use glottal stops [ʔ] to replace /t/ before vowel sounds and at the end of words: WA_TER, FI_TTING, WAI_T SOR_T OF.

- Listen and decide if the accent is GB or regional:

🎧 6.25

1. **Waiter, a pint of water, please.**   GB   Regional

2. **Have you got a lighter?**   GB   Regional

3. **Tonight's the hottest night.**   GB   Regional

4. **What a great artist**   GB   Regional

5. **Pat isn't assertive at all.**   GB   Regional

6. **What beautiful writing!**   GB   Regional

7. **It isn't wet at the moment.**   GB   Regional

8. **This pattern's complicated.**   GB   Regional

? 133

7

Approximants

are smooth, vowel-like consonant sounds made without contact.
Lateral approximants are released through the sides of the tongue.

SOUNDS	86-88	w r j
	89-90	l ɫ
Spellings	91	< l >
	92	Silent < l >
	93	Silent < r >
Linking	94	r
Activities	95	
sounds in accents	96	**r**

85

W

Spellings / Examples	Position
< w, u, o >	
well **w**ord **w**ant a**w**ake **wh**ale **wh**ether q**u**ality q**u**estion acq**u**ire pers**u**ade lang**u**age **o**ne	

))) 7.2   **Wh**y **w**on't any**o**ne **w**ish me **w**ell on my t**w**entieth?
Well, this q**u**ote by **W**ilde is q**u**ite **w**onderful.

r

Spellings / Examples	Position
< r >	
reach rose ride rash room resist arrive corrupt marry borrow write cry private grow thrill	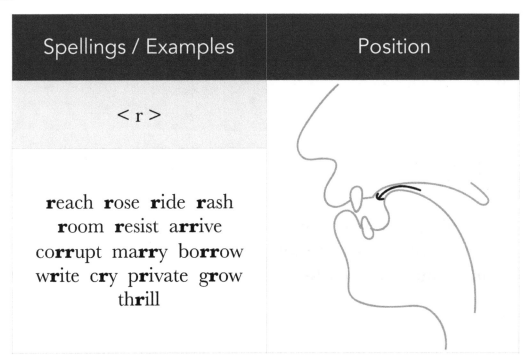

))) 7.4   **R**ain is p**r**edicted so it's **r**eally **r**isky for the **R**ed A**rr**ows. **R**ightly or w**r**ongly, **r**ents have inc**r**eased th**r**oughout B**r**itain.

j

Spellings / Examples	Position
< y, u, e >	
yes **y**olk **y**awn **y**outh **y**ear be**y**ond **u**ser **u**nison f**u**sion d**u**e val**u**e n**e**w curf**e**w	

))) 7.6   Yes, I usually queue but yesterday I refused.
A few nuisance youths were due on Tuesday.

l

Spellings / Examples	Position
< l >	
love like leave lazy less plead claim allowed olive only	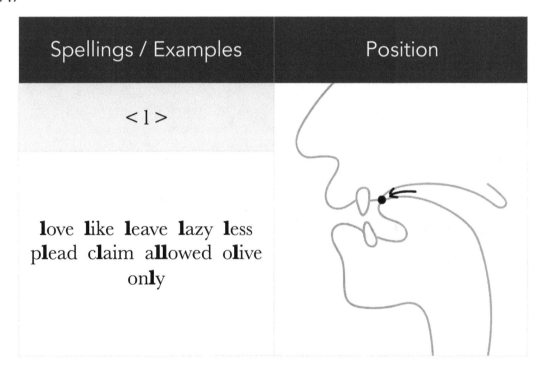

)) 7.8   Lonely and lost, Clive left England for Italy.
Please close and lock the place quickly, leave your belongings.

Spellings / Examples	Position
< l >	
fa**ll** rai**l** whi**l**e du**ll** sha**ll** specia**l** a**l**ways caro**l** sai**l**s hand**l**e	

All the people fill several halls, it's incredible!
Well, their medal's official, so we'll call them, shall we?

< l >

∩ 7.11

- *Can you hear a difference in the < l > in these words?*

nai<u>l</u>   <u>l</u>ane

? 134

---⊙---

∩ 7.12

< l > is pronounced as clear /l/ (p. 89) **before a vowel sound or /j/**.
< l > is pronounced as dark [ɫ] (p. 90) **before a consonant sound** or with **no following sound**.

---⊙---

- *Choose whether the word is pronounced with clear /l/ or dark [ɫ]:*

1. pale __[ɫ]__

2. parlour _____

3. cold _____

4. collide _____

5. clean _____

6. uncle _____

7. soul _____

8. slow _____

9. loop _____

10. pool _____

? 134))) 7.13

Silent < l >

- Match the words to their transcriptions:

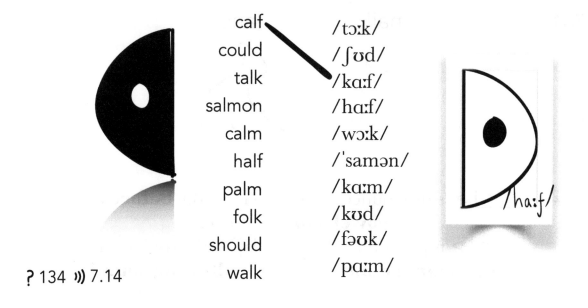

calf	/tɔːk/
could	/ʃʊd/
talk	/kɑːf/
salmon	/hɑːf/
calm	/wɔːk/
half	/ˈsamən/
palm	/kɑːm/
folk	/kʊd/
should	/fəʊk/
walk	/pɑːm/

/haːf/

? 134))) 7.14

⊙

∩ 7.15   Sometimes < l > is silent after a vowel, though there
is **no rule for when it occurs**.

⊙

- Which of the words contain a silent < l > (6 in total)?

yolk hulk colon colonel
mould would salt chalk
balm bald stalk stale

/bɔːld/

? 134
))) 7.16

Silent < r >

— Listen to these country names, which of them do not contain /r/?

🎧 7.17 No<u>r</u>way F<u>r</u>ance Qata<u>r</u> <u>R</u>ussia Tu<u>r</u>key
? 135

⊙

🎧 7.18 In GB English < r >:
- is **pronounced before a vowel sound**.
- is **silent before a consonant sound**.
- is **silent if no sound follows**.

⊙

))) 7.19 farm sir earn burn born war shore
mother persist clearly where barely

— Which words contain silent < r >?

raw worse court crate siren
sailor beer reed pair
particular internal religion
? 135
🎧 7.20 garment serial

93

Linking < r >

- *Listen to the sentence - how many < r > are pronounced?*

🎧 7.21
❓ 135

There are about four car engines over there.

⊙

🎧 7.22

In connected speech, a word ending < r > or < re > will **join to the next word with /r/ if the following word begins with a vowel sound**.

⊙

- *Which example in each line contains a linking /r/?*

1. factor fifty   (factor into)
2. far from   far away
3. there aren't   there can't
4. sir Anthony   sir Charles
5. four bananas   four apples
6. sure about   sure not
7. sister Jenny   sister Anne
8. near miss   near England
9. fair enough   fair play

❓ 135 🔊 7.23

\<r\> Activities

- Find one silent \< r \> and one linking /r/ in each sentence.

1. The fir trees are absolutely stunning.
   X
2. Where are we going?
3. I'm bored, this actor isn't very good.
4. Jane's enjoying herself in her old age.
5. I don't care, she's not coming here again.

? 135))) 7.24

- Write the animal names, they all contain silent \< r \>:

bird

? 136
))) 7.25

sounds in accents

r

🎧 7.26

In Ireland we pronounce every written < r >, so we say SHA<u>R</u>K, HO<u>R</u>SE, SPIDE<u>R</u>. This also occurs in most American & Scottish accents, but only in a few accents in England and Wales. Accents that include every 'r' are 'rhotic', those that follow the silent 'r' rule like GB English, are 'non-rhotic'.

- Are the words pronounced in a rhotic or non-rhotic accent?

🎧 7.27

1. bird _____	**2. mother** _____
3. car _____	**4. there** _____
5. aren't _____	**6. port** _____
7. park _____	**8. four** _____
9. thirst _____	**10. nearly** _____
11. worth _____	**12. tour** _____

❓ 136

Nasals

are made by releasing sound through the nose.

SOUNDS	98-100	m n ŋ
Spellings	101	< ng >
	102-103	Initial Clusters
linking	104-105	Final Clusters
	106-107	Syllabic Consonants
sounds in accents	108	ŋ

m

))) 8.1

Spellings / Examples	Position
< m >	
meet ad**m**it **m**atch i**mm**erse **m**ood **m**oist **m**are li**m**b rhyth**m** ai**m**	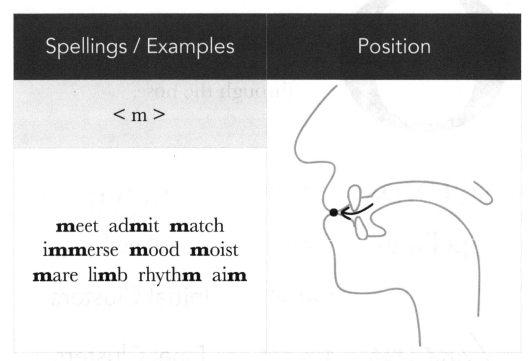

))) 8.2 **M**y thu**m**bs are nu**m**b fro**m** **m**inus te**m**peratures.
I'**m** co**m**ing ho**m**e on **M**onday **m**orning, **m**um.

n

⊙

Spellings / Examples	Position
< n >	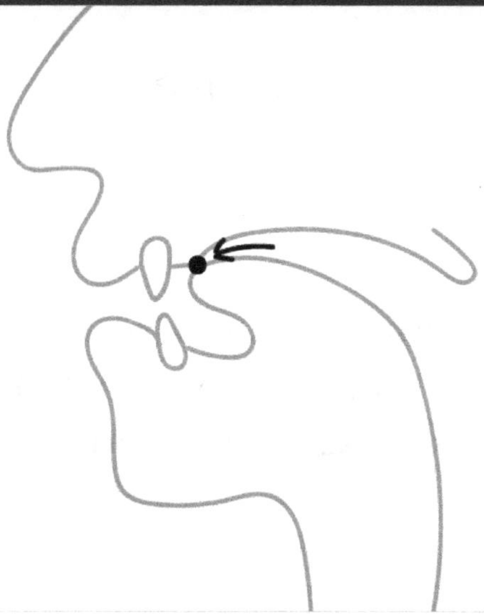
nick a**n**alysis **n**erd ba**nan**a **n**ote **n**ou**n** lea**n** sudde**n** ru**n** mi**n**d	

I **n**eed to k**n**ow whe**n** **N**aomi's pla**n**e la**n**ds.
Soo**n** you ca**n** a**nn**oy your cousi**n**s a**n**d **n**ephews.

⊙

ŋ

Spellings / Examples	Position
< ng, n >	
twinkle ba**ng** ba**n**k lu**ng** wro**ng** do**n**key worki**ng** sweepi**ng** e**n**gross i**n**clude	

)) 8.6 Tha**n**ks for bri**ng**ing your mo**n**key to E**ng**land.
I thi**n**k you're sitti**ng** on my a**n**kle, u**n**cle.

100

< ng >

- What is the difference in the pronunciation of < ng >?

⌒ 8.7

anger   hanger

? 136

—————————— ☉ ——————————

⌒ 8.8   The spelling **< ng > is pronounced /ŋ/** when it
appears at the end of a word or root word
(ha<u>ng</u>, ha<u>ng</u>er, lo<u>ng</u>ing).
< ng > is pronounced /ŋg/:
i) in the middle of a word (a<u>ng</u>er, E<u>ng</u>land).
ii) in superlatives and comparatives (lo<u>ng</u>er, lo<u>ng</u>est).

—————————— ☉ ——————————

- Circle the word in each group that contains /ŋg/:

1. finger thing winger   4. stronger strong strongly
2. hunger hanger hung   5. single singer singing
3. talking English speaking 6. long longing longest

? 136)) 8.9

Initial Clusters

- How many consonant sounds begin the following words?

🎧 8.10   saw   straw   store

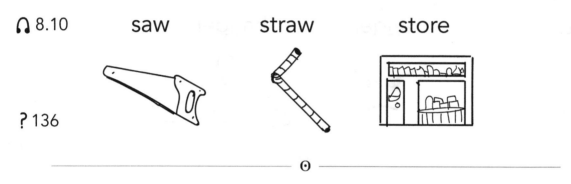

? 136

---⊙---

🎧 8.11   An English syllable can start with a vowel sound or **up to three consonants in sequence**.
More than one consonant sound pronounced in sequence is called a **consonant cluster**.

---⊙---

- Underline 3 initial consonant clusters in each sentence:

1. Such a splendid blue sky tonight!

2. Do all British swans belong to the Queen?

3. Scroll down to the climate news.

4. Have you tried this beautiful vegetable stew?

? 137))) 8.12

– *Write the words you hear into the gaps matching their clusters:*

🎧 8.13

/pl/ _____   /fr/ _____

/br/ _____   /θw/ _____

/tw/ _____   /sp/ _____

/dr/ _____   /hj/ _____

/kw/ _____   /nj/ ___*new*___

/gl/ _____   /mj/ _____

📄 137))) 8.14

– *Think of a word for each 3 consonant cluster:*

1. /spl/ _____

2. /spr/ _____

3. /spj/ _____

4. /str/ _____   /splaʃ/

5. /stj/ _____

6. /skr/ _____

7. /skw/ _____

))) 8.15 – *Repeat some options for each cluster.*

Final Clusters

- Practise the words with 2 final consonant sounds:

))) 8.16

width camp length sponge
help belt task wasp

- Add < ed > to each word to make 3 final consonant sounds:

))) 8.17

fix ask film sponge
thump grasp bulge involve

- Add < s > to each word to make 3 final consonant sounds:

))) 8.18

length realm valve gulp
lamp ninth mask hold

Θ

∩ 8.19   An English syllable can end with a cluster of **up to 4
consonant sounds**, though more than 3 is rare.
Most words that contain more than 2 final
consonant sounds have an < ed > or < s > ending.

Θ

– *Fill in the IPA crossword using the clues:*

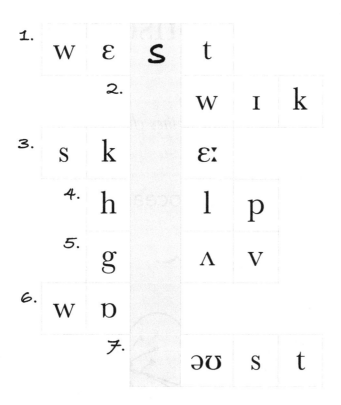

1. | w | ɛ | **s** | t |

2. | | w | ɪ | k |

3. | s | k | ɛː |

4. | h | | l | p |

5. | | g | ʌ | v |

6. | w | ɒ |

7. | | əʊ | s | t |

1. Opposite of 'east'.
2. Another word for 'fast'.
3. A symmetrical shape with 4 sides.
4. To assist with something.
5. Something you wear on your hands.
6. A clock worn on the wrist.
7. Grilled bread.

138))) 8.20

– *Write the sounds from the grey boxes into the spaces below, which word is created?*

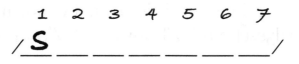

1   2   3   4   5   6   7

/ **s** __ __ __ __ __ __ /

138))) 8.21

Syllabic Consonants

- Listen to the words twice - how do they change?

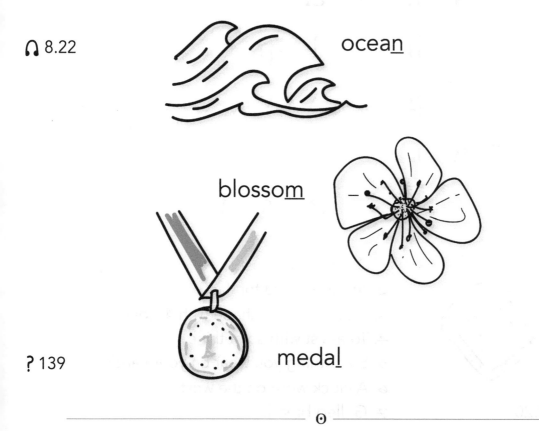

🎧 8.22

ocean

blossom

? 139

medal

⊙

🎧 8.23   The sounds /n,m,l/ can be pronounced in a syllable
without a vowel sound - a **syllabic consonant**.

In IPA transcriptions this is normally shown as /(ə)/:
/səˈdʒɛstʃ(ə)n/   /ˈbɒdɪz(ə)m/   /ˈpɑːʃ(ə)l/

⊙

- *Repeat the words using a syllabic consonant:*

))8.24   /n/ passio<u>n</u> eve<u>n</u> wouldn't liste<u>n</u>

/m/ Buddis<u>m</u> criticis<u>m</u> rhyth<u>m</u> botto<u>m</u>

/l/ hand<u>l</u>e cast<u>l</u>e financia<u>l</u>   hass<u>l</u>ing

/tɜːt(ə)l/

- *Find 2 syllabic consonants in each sentence:*

1. My conclusio<u>n</u> is that the batt<u>l</u>e is lost.

2. He's so handsome and full of passion!

3. In seven seconds the clock will chime.

4. I thought that the turtle didn't understand us!

5. We needn't worry about the animals now.

139)) 8.25

107

sounds in accents

🎧 8.26

In Milton Keynes and throughout the South East of England, in an accent known as 'Estuary', locals pronounce 'ing' endings with /n/ instead of /ŋ/: SOMETH<u>ING</u>, WORK<u>ING</u>, LONG<u>ING</u>. This actually occurs in most regional accents of English all over the world.

- Listen and decide if the accent is GB or regional:

🎧 8.27

1. Watching this isn't helping!   GB   Regional

2. Anything worth adding?   GB   Regional

3. What are you thinking of doing? GB   Regional

4. Driving without stopping   GB   Regional

5. Something out of nothing.   GB   Regional

6. I'm having a meeting at 2.   GB   Regional

? 139

Minimal Pairs

Two words that have the same pronunciation except for one sound.

Vowel Pairs

⊙

	/ɛ,a/
110	/ʌ,a/
	/ʌ,ɒ/
	/ɪ,iː/
111	/ʊ,uː/
	/ɛ,əː/
	/ʌ,əː/
	/ɒ,ɔː/
112	/a,ɑː/
	/əː,ɑː/
	/ɒ,əʊ/
	/ɔː,əʊ/
113	/ɛ,eɪ/
	/ɑː,aɪ/

Consonant Pairs

	/f,θ/
114	/θ,s/
	/v,ð/
	/s,z/
115	/z,ð/
	/s,ʃ/
	/tʃ,ʃ/
	/p,b/
116	/t,θ/
	/d,ð/
	/w,v/
117	/r,l/
	/j,dʒ/
	/n,ŋ/

⊙

))) M1　/ɛ/ vs /a/

said　lept　wreck　gem　merry　rebel　kettle
sad　lapped　rack　jam　marry　rabble　cattle

/dʒɛm/　　/dʒam/

))) M2　/ʌ/ vs /a/

tongue　sunned　uncle　budge　much　crumb　rupture
tang　　sand　　ankle　badge　match　cram　　rapture

))) M3　/ʌ/ vs /ɒ/

done　luck　crust　sudden　colour　wonder　worrier
don　　lock　crossed　sodden　collar　wander　warrior

/ɪ/ vs /iː/

fit	live	sin	itch	is	fizz	skim
feet	leave	seen	each	ease	fees	scheme

))) M5 /ʊ/ vs /uː/

soot	full	pull	hood	could	should	wood
suit	fool	pool	who'd	cooed	shooed	wooed

))) M6 /ɛ/ vs /əː/

ten	bed	west	head	death	steady	lend
turn	bird	worst	heard	dearth	sturdy	learned

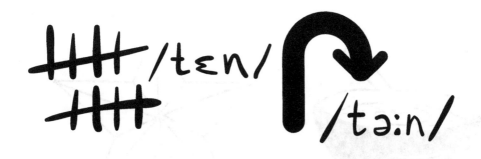

))) M7 /ʌ/ vs /əː/

shut	stun	bun	stud	cub	cut	hull
shirt	stern	burn	stirred	curb	curt	hurl

))M8 /ɒ/ vs /ɔː/

p**o**t	st**o**ck	c**o**t	p**o**d	**o**dd	f**o**nd	b**o**x
p**or**t	st**al**k	c**au**ght	p**our**ed	**oar**ed	f**aw**ned	b**aul**ks

))M9 /a/ vs /ɑː/

b**a**n	h**a**t	h**a**sh	p**a**d	**a**m	p**a**tch	**a**nt
b**ar**n	h**ear**t	h**ar**sh	p**arr**ed	**ar**m	p**ar**ch	**au**nt

))M10 /əː/ vs /ɑː/

st**ir**	h**ear**d	p**ur**se	c**ur**t	b**ir**th	p**er**k	f**ir**m
st**ar**	h**ar**d	p**a**ss	c**ar**t	b**a**th	p**ar**k	f**ar**m

/stəː/

/stɑː/

)))M11 /ɒ/ vs /əʊ/

got   rod   want sock rotter honour bossed

goat road won't soak rota   owner boast

)))M12 /ɔː/ vs /əʊ/

law   gore order fawn chalk porch soared

low   go   odour phone choke poach sewed

)))M13 /ɛ/ vs /eɪ/

edge fed wet den   special nettle heaven

age   fade wait deign spatial natal   haven

)))M14 /ɑː/ vs /ʌɪ/

arm cart bark heart tarred charm tardy

I'm   kite bike height tide   chime tidy

/Kɑːt/   /Kʌɪt/

))M15 /f/ vs /θ/

first	fought	free	four	half	deaf
thirst	thought	three	thaw	hearth	death

))M16 /θ/ vs /s/

think	theme	thumb	thigh	path	myth	worth
sink	seem	sum	sigh	pass	miss	worse

/sɪŋk/   /θɪŋk/

))M17 /v/ vs /ð/

van	vie	lava	reeves	sliver	clove
than	thy	lather	wreaths	slither	clothe

))M18 /s/ vs /z/

said   sue   face   rice   loose   use (n)   fleece
zed   zoo   phase   rise   lose   use (v)   fleas

))M19 /z/ vs /ð/

zen   whizz   breeze   lows   sues   close
then   with   breathe   loathe   soothe   clothe

))M20 /s/ vs /ʃ/

sin   seat   sore   parcel   fist   lease   mess
shin   sheet   sure   partial   fished   leash   mesh

/ʃiːt/   /siːt/

))M21 /tʃ/ vs /ʃ/

chair   cheap   chew   march   batch   watch   witch
share   sheep   shoe   marsh   bash   wash   wish

))) M22 /p/ vs /b/

pit park pole dapple harper cap rope

bit bark bowl dabble harbour cab robe

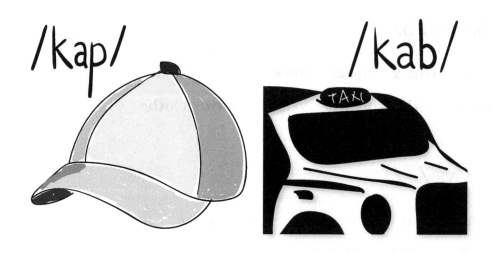

/kap/ /kab/

))) M23 /t/ vs /θ/

taught tick tour part mats heat boat

thought thick thaw path maths heath both

))) M24 /d/ vs /ð/

dare dough den doze load larder skied

there though then those loathe lather scythe

))M25 /w/ vs /v/

wary west weird wide wiser worse while

vary vest veered vied visor verse vilc

/wɛst/

w

/vɛst/

))M26 /r/ vs /l/

ram reach wrong crime fairy correct storing

lamb leech long climb fairly collect stalling

))M27 /j/ vs /dʒ/

yolk yell yet your yard yacht use (n)

joke gel jet jaw jarred jot juice

))M28 /n/ vs /ŋ/

sinner thin ban winner son sit in ran

singer thing bang winger sung sitting rang

Answer Key

⊙

⊙

Answer Key - Introduction

0.3

Thc difference between /p/, /t/ and /k/ is the place the air is blocked when they are pronounced:

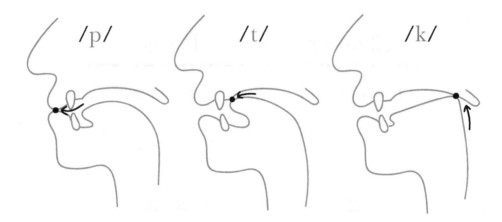

/p/   /t/   /k/

0.4

1. Bilabial   2. Labio-dental   3. Dental   4. Glottal
5. Velar   6. Alveolar

0.5

/s/ is made only using air - it is a **voiceless sound**.
/z/ is made with voice (vibration of the vocal cords in the throat) - it is a **voiced sound**.

0.7

cheese /tʃiːz/ - the < s > is pronounced /z/.
mouse /maʊs/ - the < s > is pronounced /s/.

0.8

Words with underlined voiced sound:

1. playe<u>d</u> 2. o<u>f</u> 3. fa<u>th</u>er 4. vi<u>s</u>ion 5. <u>b</u>ath
6. ri<u>dg</u>e 7. bu<u>s</u>iness a<u>ng</u>er

0.9

1. cool /uː/ (the others are pronounced with /ʊ/)
2. put /ʊ/ (the others are pronounced with /ʌ/)
3. north /ɔː/ (the others are pronounced with /əː/)
4. bother /ɒ/ (the others are pronounced with /əʊ/)
5. earn /əː/ (the others are pronounced with /ɛː/)
6. brown /aʊ/ (the others are pronounced with /əʊ/)
7. ear /ɪə/ (the others are pronounced with /ɛː/)
8. taken /ə/ (the others are pronounced with /ɪ/)
9. promise /ɒ/ (the others are pronounced with /ə/)
10. war /ɔː/ (the others are pronounced with /ɑː/)
11. tough /ʌ/ (the others are pronounced with /ɒ/)

0.10

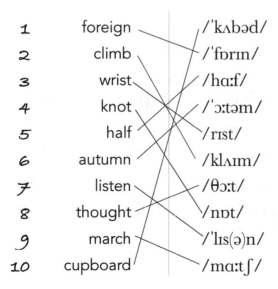

121

Silent consonant(s) are:

1. g 2. b 3. w 4. k 5. l 6. n 7. t
8. gh 9. r* 10. p & r*

The < r > is silent in GB English, though many native English speakers will pronounce these < r >, see 'Sounds in Accents', p. 96 and 'Silent < r >' p. 93.

0.13

1. WC 2. GB 3. GB 4. WC 5. GB 6. WC

Answer Key - Chapter 1

1.3

They are the same sound - /ə/:
/əˈplɔːz/ /ˈlɑːftə/ /kəˈnɛkt/ /səˈprʌɪz/

1.5

a	e	o	u
assist	perhaps	apron	surround
extra	dancer	obtain	pursuit
applaud	anthem	collect	forum
woman	lawyer	terror	suspend
collar	problem	button	spectrum

1.7

2 schwas are: 'The' /ðə/, 'for' /fə/

1.10

1. can 2. than 3. to 4. the 5. are
6. should 7. somc 8. your 9. her 10. from

1.11

A 'from' is pronounced /frɒm/ and is stressed.
B 'from' is pronounced /frəm/ and is weak.

1.13 /ə/

1. A: weak / B: strong
2. A: strong / B: weak
3. A: strong / B: weak
4. A: weak / B: strong
5. A: weak / B: strong
6. A: weak / B: strong
7. A: strong / B: weak
8. A: weak / B: strong

1.16

/ɪ/	/i/	/ə/
cott<u>a</u>ge	cos<u>y</u>	cott<u>o</u>n
shak<u>i</u>ng	shak<u>y</u>	shak<u>e</u>r
r<u>e</u>lease	reall<u>y</u>	s<u>u</u>rreal
<u>e</u>volve	voll<u>ey</u>	evoluti<u>o</u>n
wom<u>e</u>n	womanl<u>y</u>	wom<u>a</u>n

1.18

1. Di̱d yo̱u e̱njoy the̱ show?
   ɪ   u ɪ   ə

2. Ca̱n i̱t corne̱r quickly̱?
   ə ɪ   ə   i

3. Wi̱ll he̱ mana̱ge to̱ see the̱m now?
   ɪ   i   ɪ   ə   ə

4. A̱re we̱ goi̱ng to̱ do something?
   ə   i   ɪ   ə   ɪ

5. Yo̱u said i̱t wa̱s already̱ fini̱shed?
   u   ɪ ə   i   ɪ

1.19

2 pronunciations of 'to':
1. /tə/ in 'to Brazil'
2. /tu/ in 'to Argentina'

2 pronunciations of 'the':
1. /ðə/ in 'the Nigerian'
2. /ði/ in 'the Egyptian'

1.23

In both combinations the words join with /r/.

1.27

1. GB 2. Regional 3. Regional 4. GB 5. GB 6. Regional 7. Regional 8. GB

Answer Key - Chapter 2

2.13

ɪ	ʊ	ɛ
fist	shook	health
symbol	push	sell
English	could	bend
ship	stood	breath

ɒ	ʌ	a
gone	enough	land
watch	none	back
hot	sun	splash
quarrel	rush	ant

2.15

1. women   2. once   3. again   4. business   5. says
6. does   7. friend   8. built   9. flood   10. sausage

2.16

- Word construction possible answers (further rarely used words may be possible):

1. /lɪv/ LIVE   /lʌv/ LOVE
2. /bɪd/ BID   /bɛd/ BED   /bʌd/ BUD   /bad/ BAD
3. /θɪŋk/ THINK   /θaŋk/ THANK
4. /ʃʊd/ SHOULD   /ʃɛd/ SHED   /ʃɒd/ SHOD

5. /wɪtʃ/ WHICH/WITCH /wɒtʃ/ WATCH
6. /fɪl/ FILL /fʊl/ FULL /fɛl/ FELL
7. /sɪŋ/ SING /sʌŋ/ SUNG /saŋ/ SANG /sɒŋ/ SONG
8. /ʃɪp/ SHIP /ʃɒp/ SHOP

CROSSWORD

2.19

1. Regional 2. GB 3. GB 4. Regional 5. Regional
6. GB 7. Regional 8. GB

Answer Key - Chapter 3

3.13

iː	uː	əː
reach	soon	search
sheet	fruit	worth
eve	move	hurt
niece	drew	<u>jou</u>rnal
scene	route	first

ɔː	ɛː	ɑː
lawn	flare	half
door	chair	shark
sought	fairy	charm
tore	wear	bath
fall	vary	hard

3.15

1. born   2. team   3. loop   4. fair/fare   5. work   6. true
7. far   8. hard   9. sir   10. knee   11. raw/roar   12. square

3.16

1. All <u>work</u> and no play makes Jack a dull boy.
2. He's as <u>hard</u> as nails.
3. I got the <u>raw</u> end of the deal.
4. We're <u>knee</u> deep in trouble.
5. Can you keep me in the <u>loop</u>?
6. I won that game <u>fair</u> and <u>square</u>.

3.17

'beach' contains the shortest /iː/ of the three words.
'bead' contains the longest /iː/ of the three words.

3.20

1. leaf   2. fought   3. surf   4. boot   5. peace
6. half   7. torch   8. insert   9. farce   10. tooth

3.21

	word (full length)	+ /d/ (full length)	+ /t/ (reduced)
/bɔː/	bore	bored	bought
/hɜː/	her	heard/herd	hurt
/kɑː/	car	card	cart
/niː/	knee	need/knead	neat
/suː/	sue	sued	suit

3.23

Words that are pronounced /a/ instead of /ɑː/ on the recording:

aunt master gasp laugh clasp
glance sample fast task grass

Answer Key - Chapter 4

4.15

Each word is pronounced firstly with diphthong /ʊə/, secondly with long vowel /ɔː/, and thirdly with a long version of short vowel /ʊ/.

4.17

/ɔː/	long /ʊ/
sure tour	curious plural
moor surely	during pure
poor demure	puerile furious

4.19

eɪ	ɔɪ	ʌɪ
tape	boil	height
cr<u>ay</u>on	toy	tried
aim	l<u>oy</u>al	as<u>y</u>lum
break	choice	bike

əʊ	aʊ	ɪə
foam	ab<u>ou</u>t	beer
joke	vow	mat<u>e</u>rial
expl<u>o</u>sion	loud	year
pill<u>ow</u>	p<u>ow</u>er	sinc<u>e</u>re

4.21

- Word construction possible answers (further rarely used words may be possible):

1. bait /eɪ/ bite /ʌɪ/ boat /əʊ/ bout /aʊ/
2. nay, neigh /eɪ/ nigh /nʌɪ/ no, know /əʊ/ now /aʊ/ near /ɪə/
3. flay /eɪ/ fly /ʌɪ/ flow /əʊ/
4. play /eɪ/ ploy /ɔɪ/ ply /ʌɪ/ plough /aʊ/
5. spy /ʌɪ/ spear /ɪə/
6. drain /eɪ/ drone /əʊ/ drown /aʊ/
7. toy /ɔɪ/ tie, Thai /ʌɪ/ toe, tow /əʊ/ tear /ɪə/
8. main, mane /eɪ/ mine /ʌɪ/ moan /əʊ/

4.22

1. "so so" /əʊ/   2. "pay day" /eɪ/   3. "hear hear" /ɪə/
4. "high time" /ʌɪ/   5. "out and out" /aʊ/
6. "hoity toity" /ɔɪ/

4.25

	GB	Geordie	Scouse
A. No, I don't know.	2	1	3
B. Row the boat, Tony.	1	3	2
C. Both roads are slow.	3	2	1
D. I'm so lonely on my own.	2	3	1
E. Phone me at home, ok?	1	2	3

Answer Key - Chapter 5

5.11

1. hon<u>ou</u>r 2. ex<u>h</u>ibition 3. <u>h</u>eir 4. ve<u>h</u>icle
5. <u>gh</u>ost 6. stoma<u>ch</u> 7. s<u>h</u>epherd 8. <u>h</u>onest
9. <u>wh</u>isper 10. ex<u>h</u>austed

5.12

1. wor<u>th</u> /θ/ 2. wea<u>th</u>er /ð/ 3. four<u>th</u> /θ/
4. fur<u>th</u>er /ð/ 5. <u>th</u>ese /ð/ 6. <u>th</u>eory /θ/
7. pa<u>th</u> /θ/ 8. pa<u>ths</u> /ð/ 9. ba<u>th</u>e /ð/ 10. ba<u>th</u> /θ/

5.13

<u>sh</u>ell ʃ	<u>th</u>ank θ	lau<u>gh</u> f
pa<u>c</u>e s	ero<u>s</u>ion ʒ	bo<u>th</u>er ð
ra<u>v</u>e v	choo<u>s</u>e z	<u>h</u>ot h

5.14

1. /nəʊz/ nose knows
2. /sɔː/ sore saw
3. /pɔːz/ pause paws
4. /θruː/ through threw
5. /ˈsteɪʃ(ə)n(ə)ri/ stationery stationary
6. /hɛː/ hare hair
7. /ʃɪə/ shear sheer
8. /θrəʊn/ thrown throne
9. /siːz/ seize seas/sees
10. /ðɛː/ there their/they're

5.16

'lock<u>s</u>' is pronounced with voiceless /s/, 'log<u>s</u>' is pronounced with voiced /z/.

5.19

1. sticks /s/ 2. stones /z/ 3. slabs /z/ 4. slaps /s/
5. theirs /z/ 6. thats /s/ 7. things /z/ 8. thinks /s/
9. knows /z/ 10. laughs /s/

5.23

1. Regional 2. GB 3. GB 4. Regional
5. GB 6. Regional 7. Regional 8. GB

Answer Key - Chapter 6

6.11

a) /ˈnɒt/ 6 (k)   *b)* /rɪˈsiːt/ 5 (p)
c) /ˈbaleɪ/ 7 (t)   *d)* /ˈwɛnzdeɪ/ 4 (d)
e) /ˈniː/ 9 (k)   *f)* /ˈsanwɪtʃ/ 8 (d)
g) /ˈθʌm/ 3 (b)   *h)* /ˈkəʊm/ 1 (b)
i) /ˈkɑːs(ə)ɬ/ 10 (t) *j)* /ˈnəʊm/ 2 (g)

- Silent letter in each word is in brackets.

6.12

The < t > in 'lightning' is pronounced differently.

6.15

The < t > that could be pronounced [ʔ] is <u>underlined</u>:

1. I<u>t</u> was true!
2. Time to ge<u>t</u> back!
3. Wha<u>t</u> type of cat is it?
4. Can't I si<u>t</u> here?
5. Talk abou<u>t</u> wasting water!
6. Absolu<u>t</u>ely not!

6.16

'stop<u>ed</u>' and 'finish<u>ed</u>' are pronounced /t/.
'paus<u>ed</u>' is pronounced /d/.
'start<u>ed</u>' is pronounced /ɪd/.

6.19

/t/	/d/	/ɪd/
shopped ripped	poured bailed	afforded boasted
messed fished	booed sewed	raided bloated
washed fetched	pleased arranged	needed carted
licked trekked	loaned robbed	herded alluded

6.22

1. dogged   2. blessed   3. naked   4. crooked   5. beloved
6. learned   7. wicked   8. sacred

6.25

1. Regional   2. GB   3. Regional   4. Regional   5. GB
6. Regional   7. GB   8. Regional

Answer Key - Chapter 7

7.11

'nail' is pronounced with [ɫ] - known as 'dark l'.
'lane' is pronounced with /l/ - known as 'clear l'.

7.13

1. pale [ɫ]   2. parlour /l/   3. cold [ɫ]   4. collide /l/
5. clean /l/   6. uncle [ɫ]   7. soul [ɫ]   8. slow /l/
9. loop /l/   10. pool [ɫ]

7.14

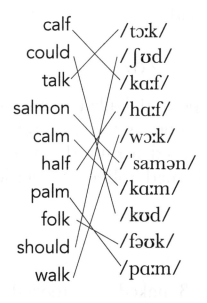

calf   /tɔːk/
could   /ʃʊd/
talk   /kɑːf/
salmon   /hɑːf/
calm   /wɔːk/
half   /ˈsamən/
palm   /kɑːm/
folk   /kʊd/
should   /fəʊk/
walk   /pɑːm/

7.16

The following words contain silent < l >:

yolk colonel would chalk balm stalk

7.17

'Norway', 'Qatar' & 'Turkey' do not contain /r/.

7.20

The following words contain silent < r >:

worse   court   sailor   beer   pair
particular   internal   garment

7.21

In the audio, the **<u>bold, underlined</u>** < r > are pronounced:

The**r**e a**r**e about four ca**r** engines over there.

7.23

The following sentences contain linking /r/:

1. factor into   2. far away   3. there aren't
4. sir Anthony   5. four apples   6. sure about
7. sister Anne   8. near England   9. fair enough

7.24

silent < r > = ✗   linking /r/ = ‿

   1. The fir trees are absolutely stunning.

   2. Where are we going?

   3. I'm bored, this actor isn't very good.

   4. Jane's enjoying herself in her old age.

   5. I don't care, she's not coming here again.

7.25

bird scorpion worm shark butterfly horse lizard

7.27

1. rhotic 2. non-rhotic 3. non-rhotic 4. rhotic
5. non-rhotic 6. rhotic 7. rhotic 8. non-rhotic
9. rhotic 10. non-rhotic 11. non-rhotic 12. rhotic

Answer Key - Chapter 8

8.7

'a<u>n</u>ger' is pronounced /ŋg/
'ha<u>ng</u>er' is pronounced /ŋ/

8.9

The word that contains /ŋg/ is:

1. finger 2. hunger 3. English 4. stronger
5. single 6. longest

8.10

'saw' - one consonant sound /s/ at the beginning.
'straw' - three consonant sounds /str/ at the beginning.
'store' - two consonant sounds /st/ at the beginning.

8.12

1. Such a <u>spl</u>endid <u>bl</u>ue <u>sky</u> tonight! /spl/ /bl/ /sk/
2. Do all <u>Br</u>itish <u>sw</u>ans belong to the <u>Qu</u>een? /br/ /sw/ kw/
3. <u>Scr</u>oll down to the <u>cl</u>imate <u>n</u>ews. /skr/ /kl/ /nj/
4. Have you <u>tr</u>ied this <u>beau</u>tiful vegetable <u>stew</u>? /tr/ /bj/ /stj/

8.13

/pl/	please	/fr/	free
/br/	break	/θw/	thwart
/tw/	twin	/sp/	spark
/dr/	drink	/hj/	human
/kw/	quick	/nj/	new
/gl/	glow	/mj/	mute

8.15

/spl/ split splash splendid
/spr/ spring spread sprout
/spj/ spew dispute
/str/ strong stress street
/stj/ student stew steward
/skr/ script scream scratch
/skw/ squeal square squid

8.20

1. west   s

2. quick   k

3. square   w

4. help   ɛ

5. glove   l

6. watch   tʃ

7. toast   t

8.21

/skwɛltʃt/

The word is 'squelched' - the past participle of the verb 'to squelch', which is the sound made when walking through mud.

It is one syllable and contains 7 sounds; only a very small number of English syllables contain so many sounds.

8.22

In the second pronunciation of each word, the vowel sound is not pronounced in the second syllable.

8.25

    1. My conclusio<u>n</u> is that the batt<u>l</u>e is lost.

    2. He's so handso<u>m</u>e and full of passio<u>n</u>!

    3. In seve<u>n</u> seco<u>n</u>ds the clock will chime.

    4. I thought that the turt<u>l</u>e did<u>n</u>'t understand us!

    5. We need<u>n</u>'t worry about the anima<u>l</u>s now.

8.27

1. Regional 2. GB 3. GB 4. Regional
5. GB 6. Regional